Greater Than a Tourist
Tenerife
Canary Islands
Spain

50 Travel Tips from a Local

Ana M. Ionita

Order Information: To order this title please email lbrenenc@gmail.com or visit

GreaterThanATourist.com. A bulk discount can be provided.

Lock Haven, PA
All rights reserved.
ISBN: 9781521877944

>TOURIST

50 TRAVEL TIPS FROM A LOCAL

Ana M. Ionita

BOOK DESCRIPTION

Are you excited about planning your next trip?

Do you want to try something new while traveling?

Would you like some guidance from a local?

If you answered yes to any of these questions, then this book is just for you. Greater Than a Tourist- Tenerife Canary Islands Spain by Ana M. Ionita offers the inside scope on Tenerife. Most travel books tell you how to travel like a tourist. Although there's nothing wrong with that, as a part of the Greater than a Tourist series, this book will give you travel tips from someone who lives at your next travel destination. In these pages you'll discover local advice that will help you throughout your stay. This book will not tell you exact addresses or store hours but instead will give you an excitement and knowledge from a local that you may not find in other smaller print travel books. Travel like a local. Slow down, stay in one place, and get to know the people and the culture of a place. By the time you finish this book, you will be eager and prepared to travel to your next destination.

Ana M. Ionita

TABLE OF CONTENTS

13. Practice Senderismo in Anaga Park

14. Dine on Tapas

15. Spend a Relaxing Afternoon on a Charming Golf Course

16. Have a Delicious Steak at El Cordero

17. Have Dinner with an Unforgettable View

18. Party Like a Local

19. Eat Delicious Seafood

20. Swim in a Natural Pool

21. Indulge Yourself with the Best Ice Cream on the Island

22. Visit a Local Market

23. Snorkel with the Huge Turtles in El Puertito

24. Explore the Peculiar Mount Teide

25. Wander Around the Streets of the Old Capital

26. Tour a Vineyard

27. Drink a Cold Dorada on the Beach

28. Eat a Traditional Local Dish

29. Get Rid of All Inhibitions on a Nude Beach

30. Have a "Chupito" after a Delicious Meal

31. Take in The Islands' Best Views From The Best "Mirador"

32. Go Fishing

WHERE WILL YOU TRAVEL TO NEXT?

DEDICATION

This book is dedicated to my parents for their encouragement and support, and to my boyfriend. Without him the "Island of Eternal Spring" wouldn't be my home.

Ana M. Ionita

ABOUT THE AUTHOR

Ana M. Ionita is a writer by day and reader by night, who lives in Santa Cruz de Tenerife.

A spirited traveler, passionate cook and art enthusiast, Ana moved in Tenerife in 2015 after exploring the beauty of London. She left the busy city life with its amalgam of cultural and artistic events, embracing a simple life on the "island of eternal spring".

She never thought that the agitated city girl who was always searching for something could fall for the peace of mind "sold" by the island. But she did, becoming the island girl she never thought she would be.

Ana M. Ionita

HOW TO USE THIS BOOK

This book was written by someone who has lived in an area for over three months. The author has made the best suggestions based on their own experiences in the area. Please check that these places are still available before traveling to the area. The goal of this book is to help travelers either dream or experience different locations by providing opinions from a local.

Ana M. Ionita

FROM THE PUBLISHER

Traveling can be one of the most important moments in a person's life. The memories that you have of anticipating going somewhere new or getting to travel are some of the best. As a publisher of the Greater Than a Tourist book series, as well as the popular 50 Things to Know book series, we strive to help you learn about new places, spark your imagination, and inspire you.

Thought this book you will find something for every traveler. Wherever you are and whatever you do I wish you safe fun, and inspiring travel.

Lisa Rusczyk Ed. D.

CZYK Publishing

Ana M. Ionita

WELCOME TO > TOURIST

Ana M. Ionita

INTRODUCTION

Known as the "island of eternal spring", Tenerife is one of the seven charming Canary Islands. Famous for the Teide volcano, for its fascinating microclimate, the relaxing beaches, and the incredible landscapes, Tenerife is a little paradise on earth for people who want to unplug and enjoy the warm sun, the reinvigorating breeze, and tasty food and wine.

The most popular holiday destinations are the touristy resorts in Playa de Las Americas and Los Cristianos. However, Tenerife is much more than these areas. And in order to get closer to the real spirit of the island, all visitors should learn how to holiday like a local in Tenerife.

Ana M. Ionita

1. When to Visit Tenerife

Tenerife is known as the island of eternal spring for having incredible weather during the whole year. You can visit the island whenever you want and have a great time, without being afraid of cold weather. The lowest temperature I experienced was in January, when there were 19 Celsius degrees, which is not so bad, is it?

The warmest months are July and August and the wettest is December, but there are many people celebrating Christmas and New Year's Eve on the Canarian beaches.

Personally, I would travel to the island during the cold months, because there aren't too many places in Europe where you can spend time on the beach in winter!

2. How to Get Around

Tenerife is a small island, with two airports, an impressive number of buses and even two tram lines in its beautiful capital, Santa Cruz. However, the best way to travel around the island is by car. If you don't have a driver's license you can move around using the bus, but it is definitely slower and it doesn't give you the chance to properly explore the hidden corners of the island.

This is why renting a car is the best option. You can reserve the car before your arrival, or easily get it from the airport or your hotel. Just make sure you choose a powerful one because most of the time you'll be driving up the hills.

3. Where to Stay

Tenerife is continuously developing, and so are its touristic areas. However, in order to have an unforgettable authentic experience, staying in a hotel in the south of the island should be avoided. My suggestion is to rent an apartment from a local in a less touristy area. I would recommend travelers to use websites where people advertise their homes and choose an apartment based on their own desires. There are many apartments located exactly on the beach, and there are some superb lofts up the hill with splendid views.

You can also spend a few days in the mountains, in one of the Canarian "fincas" (farms), where you can enjoy fascinating views, interesting vegetation and delicious homemade food.

The area you choose also depends on your own desires. But no matter what part of Tenerife you select, you will probably wander around the whole island. Just keep in mind that the southern you go, the more touristy it becomes.

4. Have a Picnic in a Gorgeous "Zonas Recreativa"

Tenerife is not all about beaches and sunbathing. Local people really love spending time in the middle of nature and having great meals outdoor with their friends and family. There are many areas created for barbeques and picnics, known as "zonas recreativas". Located in the forests, these areas offer visitors not only barbeques and tables but also play areas and camping sites.

The picnic zones are empty during the week, but if you go on a Sunday they are overflowing with locals and their happy families. Canarian people's picnics are actually immense feasts, where besides indulging themselves with delicious food, people sing and dance, creating the atmosphere of a real outdoor party.

5. Sunbathe on the Golden Saharan Sand

Though most of the beaches where locals in Tenerife love going to are made of black sand, there is one special place loved by both travelers and locals. Playa de Las Teresitas is located in the north of the island, just outside the charming Santa Cruz.

Even though you will be playing with your feet in golden sand imported from Sahara, Playa de Las Teresitas is actually considered an authentic local beach and is always full of Santa Cruceros who read, relax and even exercise, making the beach their gym.

6. Learn How to Surf in El Médano

El Médano is a small charming town, full of surfers, excellent restaurants and many shops, located in the south of Tenerife. With fewer tourists than Las Americas or Los Cristianos, this little town is considered a surfing paradise. Important competitions like The Surfing World Cup have been held in El Médano, and the reason is the reinvigorating wind that almost never stops blowing.

If you want to feel adventurous and have the ultimate surfing experience, this is definitely the best place to start learning how to use the board. The Canarian surf instructors are very patient and professional so you'll be in really good hands!

7. Relax Your Mind and Body While Doing Yoga on the Beach

Canarian people love spending time outside and sometimes they ditch the sweaty gyms for exercising on the beach. Some just enjoy jogging in the morning, others do their regular exercise in the afternoon, and others, like myself, couldn't live without a relaxing session of yoga in the evening.

You can just grab your yoga mat and find a nice spot on a quiet beach, or you can join a class and enjoy group yoga and meditation with passionate locals. My favorite beach for yoga is the small "playa" in Candelaria, a nice town located close to Santa Cruz.

8. Explore an Authentic Black Sand Beach

Most visitors spend their vacations relaxing on touristy beaches in Las Americas or Los Cristianos, but the truth is that locals never set foot in these areas. The "real" beaches of the island are the black, volcanic sand ones and many of them are not famous, or very easy to get to.

Playa Bollullo is the most accessible of the stunning black sand beaches. However, in order to get there, you have to drive along a small, single track road. Or, if you feel adventurous you can walk through a banana plantation from Puerto de la Cruz until you get to the charming beach. The truth is that the beautiful wilderness of this piece of sand makes it worth the drive and even the hike.

9. Get Wet and Wild at Siam Park

Featuring a Siamese theme and claiming to be the most amazing water attraction in Europe, Siam Park is one of those places where, even though it's always full of tourists, local people like to go and have some fun.

The park is located in the south of the island and it is always packed with kids and adults who are excited to try the 29 amazing rides. Personally, I got pretty scared of most water slides but a large number of kids who were having fun gave me courage!

As I said, it can be very crowded and in order to make sure you won't stay in lines the whole day, a Fast Pass is needed.

10. Have the Ultimate Carnival Experience in Santa Cruz

With 14 public holidays and fiestas, it's almost impossible not to attend a party when visiting beautiful Tenerife. While there are many amazing fiestas, the biggest and the most fascinating is definitely the Santa Cruz de Tenerife Carnival, in February.

In order to imagine what the carnival in Tenerife is like, let me tell you that Santa Cruz won a Guinness Record for the number of people dancing under the stars. No joke, in 1987, the Cuban singer, Celia Cruz made over 250 000 shake their bodies like Latin queens in the city center! For almost two weeks, a delicious mix of Latino music, crazy costumes and glitter together with drinks and mouth-watering food makes people in Santa Cruz unleash their party animal instincts. Everybody sings and dances not caring whether it is day or night.

Ana M. Ionita

"After a visit to the beach, it's hard to

believe that we live in a material world."

Pam Shaw

Ana M. Ionita

11. Be Part of the Romería de San Isidro in Orotava

Orotava is one of the most popular historic towns in Tenerife. Not only is it worth visiting, but if you have the chance, you should celebrate Romería de San Isidro together with the people of Orotava.

Celebrated on the Sunday following the Corpus Christi fiestas, San Isidro's most popular events are the pilgrimage and the livestock fair.

The multitude of oxen that pull decorated carts, together with locals who wear traditional costumes, and their beautifully decorated balconies and windows make this celebration an amazement for the eyes of locals and travelers from all over the world.

12. Try Stand Up Paddle Boarding

Paddle boarding is one of the sports that rapidly became popular amongst locals of the charming Tenerife island. What you have to do is stand on a large surf board and paddle around using a long oar.

Does this sound easy? Well, wait for the waves to hit you! If you want to go on this adventure, you can do it in most beach towns, but the best place for water sports remains El Médano.

13. Practice Senderismo in Anaga Park

Though many locals are into water sports, senderismo, or as you might know it, hiking, is also something they love doing. There are many incredible routes and the best part is that all of them offer hikers the most amazing views.

Whether you go to the Parque Nacional de Las Cañadas del Teide (National Park of Las Canadas), or you want to explore Anaga Park, you should choose the difficulty level and the distance of the hike considering your own capacities. If you are a beginner, the best choice is, the Sendero de Los Sentidos (Path of the Senses) in the Anaga Rural Park.

Anaga Park is one of the most beautiful areas of the island, offering hikers not only the chance to get in touch with a magical natural environment but also the opportunity to see some of the best landscapes on the island. Just try to find a local guide, instead of booking a tour specially created for tourists.

14. Dine on Tapas

Tapas aren't traditional in the Canary Islands, but they are definitely a popular way to have dinner in Tenerife. There are few restaurants where they don't serve their own types of tapas, and there are even fewer ones where papas arrugadas con mojo aren't on the menu. These are salty boiled potatoes with Canarian sauces and they are served as tapas, but also as sides to almost every dish. Complete your tapas dinner with a delicious grilled octopus and some flavorful chopitos, which are deep-fried baby squids. Just avoid the restaurants on the beaches of Las Americas, Los Cristianos, or Playa de Fañabé because most of them are tourist traps.

One of my favourite tapas restaurants is D'Tapas, 26 located in Santa Cruz. With a lovely décor inside, a charming terrace and outstanding tapas created by passionate chefs, eating here is definitely a must when visiting Tenerife's capital.

15. Spend a Relaxing Afternoon on a Charming Golf Course

Tenerife is famous for the great golf courses located throughout the island. Travelers from all over the world come to this charming piece of land to take advantage of these beautifully arranged golf courses. While most of them choose to play in the south at Golf del Sur in San Miguel de Abona and Golf Costa Adeje, locals prefer the courses at Golf Buenavista del Norte. So, if you like playing golf but you don't want to stay in the touristy south, this is where you should go.

The 18 hole, a 72-par-course, has a length of 6.019 meters and it is suitable for all standards, offering reasonable rates and an incredible ocean view.

16. Have a Delicious Steak at El Cordero

Guachinches are traditional restaurants that are usually set up in someone's yard, at their farm and even in their garage. El Cordero is one of the best guachinche restaurants in Tenerife.

Located in the middle of a banana plantation, El Cordero offers foodies an authentic Tenerife experience not only through its food, but also thanks to the exquisite location and the traditional atmosphere.

The menu is not too varied and the wine is always homemade. If you love beef, order the famous T-bone. Just make sure you are really hungry or you find a partner to share it with, because its size is overwhelming. Also, don't miss having a tasty banana from the house!

17. Have Dinner with an Unforgettable View

Sunset 290 is a great place, famous among romantic people for its views, tasty dishes and the overall inviting atmosphere. Surrounded by breathtaking cliffs and overlooking the ocean this is one of the best places for people who want to have dinner while gazing at a beautiful sunset.

I honestly recommend the salads, as well as the mouthwatering cakes! And if you are a meat lover don't even think about not ordering the tasty steak. The best time to go is obviously in the evening to let yourself amazed by the beauty of the sunset.

18. Party Like a Local

While young tourists who like to party go to Veronicas strip in Las Americas, locals prefer the parties in the north part of the island. Calle De La Noria in Santa Cruz is where you should go if you want to spend a wild night out, like a local.

Calle De La Noria is a traffic free street full of restaurants, bars and clubs where you can enjoy a tasty meal during the day and attend a great party during the night.

19. Eat Delicious Seafood

Foodies from all over the world come to Tenerife to indulge themselves with the mouth-watering seafood. There is an impressive number of restaurants where they serve incredible fish, squids, octopus and other delicacies. However, one of the locals' favorite restaurant is La Cofradia de Caletillas.

Located in Candelaria, a small non-touristic town in the north part of the island, the restaurant is far from being glamorous or elegant. It looks like a normal tavern with nothing special, except the food and its location, right in front of the blue ocean.

It is one of the busiest restaurants I have ever seen, with the best fish I have ever eaten. Freshly caught and brought every morning from the hardworking fishermen, the fish is cooked with passion and served by friendly staff.

20. Swim in a Natural Pool

Swimming in the refreshing waters of the Atlantic ocean is an excellent way to begin a lovely day in Tenerife. However, your swimming experience is definitely enhanced when diving into one of the charming natural pools created without any human intervention.

One of the best natural pool is La Laja, located in San Juan de la Rambla, a historical village in the north of Tenerife.
Not only is this a great place to go for a swim, but you can also wander around the village and get in touch with its intersecting history.

In addition, there are a few traditional restaurants where the best food is served in a very relaxed atmosphere. So if you add a great meal to the refreshing swimming session and the encounter with history, you get a perfect day!

Ana M. Ionita

"How inappropriate to call this planet

Earth when it is clearly Ocean."

Arthur C. Clarke

Ana M. Ionita

21. Indulge Yourself with the Best Ice Cream on the Island

The warm weather in Tenerife makes you crave for cold drinks and ice cream all the time. I am an ice cream lover and I have always been, so I am very familiar with the places where they have the best products.

I would strongly recommend Heladeria El Sueño, located in Candelaria, a quiet town hidden from tourists. The ice cream shop is located in front of the ocean, so not only will you have the best flavors on the island but you will also have a fantastic view!

22. Visit a Local Market

With traditional market stalls full of vegetables, meat and other local products, the local market in Santa Cruz also includes a fish market and economical eateries, offering locals and visitors a fascinating shopping experience.

Named Nuestra Señora de África, this is a great outdoor market where you can find everything you need. It bustles with locals and travelers who lose themselves in the delightful mixture of flavors and colors, eager to buy fresh local products.
If you want an authentic experience, go as early as possible!

23. Snorkel with the Huge Turtles in El Puertito

El Puertito is a quiet beach away from the busy southern places. Without offering anything touristic, here is the place for people who want to ditch the sunbeds for the traditional towels on the sand and who prefer swimming and snorkeling instead of sipping cocktails and listening to loud music.

Also, this is the place for people who want to see the huge turtle families that live in the clear waters of the ocean. So, grab your snorkeling glasses and get ready for an outstanding experience!

24. Explore the Peculiar Mount Teide

Mount Teide is definitely one of the main attractions in Tenerife, so no visitor can miss seeing the unique scenery of this volcano.

You can either book a tour and see the famous mountain in the traditional touristic manner, or you can explore the volcanic trails with a local guide who will show you the way to to the highest peak in Spain.

If you choose to go up the mountain using a car, keep in mind that you can only drive until you get to the cable car, which stands at 2,356 m above the sea level. Then, you have to go with the cable car to the Upper Station, which is located at 3,555 m altitude. This is the point where three amazing hiking routes start. Are you courageous enough to begin hiking?

25. Wander Around the Streets of the Old Capital

San Cristobal de La Laguna is one of the most beautiful cities in Tenerife. It used to be the capital of the island until Santa Cruz became the main city, and it was declared World Heritage Site by UNESCO in 1999.

Its beauty is incontestable and so is its liveliness. Full of young people who go to university in this city, hip cafes and charming restaurants, the streets of La Laguna paint a memorable image for all visitors.

Wander around this beautiful city and have a cup of coffee at one of the best cafes on the island, La Cafeina.

26. Tour a Vineyard

Locals love their Dorada beer and they definitely enjoy having one or two chupitos (shots), but they are also very fond of their tasty local wine.

However, this shouldn't be a surprise since there is an impressive number of award-winning wines produced in Tenerife. So, if you are a wine lover and you want to see an authentic vineyard, you are definitely in the right place.

Not only will you get to see how the best wine comes to life, but a typical tour ends with a memorable wine tasting experience, which is always accompanied by samples of delicious local bread and cheese.

My favorite vineyard on the island is Bodega Cueva del Rey in Garachico, a beautiful historical village on the west part of the island.

27. Drink a Cold Dorada on the Beach

Dorada is the local beer and the favorite drink of all locals and travelers, especially during summer.

Produced by The Compañía Cervecera de Canarias, a brewery based in Santa Cruz de Tenerife, Dorada represents the taste of the island for all beer lovers.

You can always enjoy a cold Cerveza at a nice terrace, but to make the most out of it, grab a cold Dorada and enjoy it on one of the local beaches.

28. Eat a Traditional Local Dish

At the beginning you might tend to believe that the only culinary experience you are going to have in Tenerife involves grilled or fried seafood. This very far from being true! Canarian cuisine is an important part of all locals' lives. Known for its freshness and simplicity, the food in Tenerife is absolutely delicious.

You can begin a normal meal with a variety of tasty local cheeses, continue with a mouth-watering fish soup (Caldo de Pescado) and then ask for "Ropa Viejas", which literally mean dirty clothes and it's a dish made with beef and chicken mixed with potatoes and chickpeas. Absolutely amazing!

29. Get Rid of All Inhibitions on a Nude Beach

Far away from all touristic spots, in the north of the island, hidden by rocks, you will find a charming 250m long black sand beach. Besides the natural beauty of the place, what will amaze your eyes is the lack of inhibition that makes people stay naked on the soft sand.

Playa de Las Gaviotas is charming, the waves are inviting and the atmosphere is really relaxed.

However, if you don't feel as relaxed as the atmosphere here, you don't have to worry because you can keep the swimsuit on!

30. Have a "Chupito" after a Delicious Meal

Whether you are it is banana liquor or another kind of liquor, being offered a shot (known as chupito) from the house is something common after lunch or dinner in Tenerife. In some places, they even leave you the bottle so you can have as many chupitos as you want.

Tourists prefer Ron Miel, although locals only drink it when they have a cold. My favorite is a shot of caramel flavored vodka, but I never refuse Ron Miel, either.

Ana M. Ionita

"Our memories of the ocean will linger on, long after our footprints in the sand are gone."

Unknown Author

Ana M. Ionita

31. Take in The Islands' Best Views From The Best "Mirador"

Tenerife is not only famous for its beautiful beaches and incredible parks, but also for the unforgettable views that can make even the coldest heart melt.

There are so many viewing points that I would need to write a book only about those. However, my favorite has always been the "Mirador de Las Teresitas", a viewing point just above the local beach Las Teresitas.

The amalgam of inspiring colors, the beauty of the ocean, close to the sandy beach with its green trees, and the imposing rock makes everything look like painted on a piece of canvas.

32. Go Fishing

With more 500 fish species Tenerife is a paradise for all fishing enthusiasts. Whether you plan to rent a boat or you want to take your fishing rod and sit on the pier or on a rock, you should first obtain a fishing permit.

There are plenty of good fishing spots on the island, and many places where you can rent fishing boats from. Of course, you also need a license for a boat.

33. Experience the Night of San Juan

There is an impressive number of celebrations in Tenerife and most of them are really different from what you've seen before. One of my favorite nights of the year is the night of San Juan. San Juan is a festival celebrated on the 23rd of June, every year. In this magical night, people of the island welcome the summer season, in an incredible manner, with bonfires and music on the beach.

The party lasts until the next day and bathing in the ocean after midnight is mandatory. Also, sleeping on the beach and waiting for the sun to rise are recommended. Locals even set up their tents, to make sure they don't leave until the next day.

34. Start Your Day with a Coffee and a Mixed Croissant

Having coffee and a mixed croissant or a tasty "bocadillo" is something mandatory for every local. Breakfast is the best way to begin a productive day, isn't it?

So go to a local coffee shop, order Café cortado and a mixed croissant and get ready for another beautiful day. The mixed croissant has ham and cheese, while the small sandwich, known as " bocadillo" is made with various products. If you prefer having a sandwich, go for one with Spanish tortilla or with Jamón serrano and cheese.

35. Dance until the Sun Comes Up

Canarian people love to party. Even though they usually prefer to go out in restaurants and bars in order to drink and eat until late, they also love going to clubs from time to time.

One of the best clubs in Tenerife is Papagayo, a fantastic beach club located in the south of the island. With good music, tasty drinks and a fantastic atmosphere, this is definitely the place you should go to when in the mood to dance until the sun comes up. And the great part is that since it's located exactly on the beach, you can even enjoy a great sunrise after a wild night.

36. Souvenirs to Bring Home

A vacation is never complete until the bags are full of lovely souvenirs. Depending on what you like, there are many types of things you can bring home from this beautiful island. For instance, if you love beauty products, there are many fabrics where aloe vera is transformed into soaps, gels and creams. This would make a great gift for your mother, your sister or your girlfriend.

For foodies, you can buy tasty Canarian wines, cheese and a variety of mojos (sauces).

In addition, jewelry made of volcanic rock, as well as beautiful pearls, would definitely be the most special souvenirs from Tenerife.

And, of course, there are many typical souvenir shops where you can find all kinds of typical objects, interesting T-shirts and many other things you can choose from.

37. Where to Do Grocery Shopping

There are many local markets in Tenerife but sometimes it is faster and easier to do your grocery shopping in a supermarket. Mercadona is one of the supermarkets preferred by locals, not only because it offers a variety of products but the prices are also quite friendly. This is a 100% Spanish supermarket with stores throughout the island.

And if there isn't one near you, it is impossible not to find one of the markets operated by DinoSol. The most popular is HiperDino, a supermarket with great products and fair prices. Just stay away from the El Corte Inglés because, even though it offers a variety if qualitative products, it is extremely expensive.

38. Visit the Charming Puerto de La Cruz

Located in the northern part of the island, Puerto de la Cruz is a city everybody who comes to Tenerife should see. With its charming Martiánez Pools, the beautiful Jardín Beach, as well as the fascinating Botanical Garden, this adorable city attracts travelers from all over the world.

In addition to wandering around its beautifully arranged streets and shopping in the duty-free stores, Puerto de la Cruz gives you the chance to eat in some of the best restaurants on the island.

A strongly recommended restaurant is Bodega Julian. This family-owned tavern offers delicious food in an outstanding atmosphere. If you are lucky you can even listen to the owner and his beautiful wife's live music performance.

39. Eat Mouth-watering Lobster at "La Langostera"

People who love eating seafood are the happiest when visiting Tenerife. Whether you like oysters, crabs, prawns or lobsters, you can find the most delicious products on this charming island.

I am a foodie and I am truly in love with anything that comes from the sea. And lobster is definitely something I would never say no to. The best place to have a delicious lobster is La Langostera, a beautiful restaurant located in Los Abrigos.

The menu is rich, offering a variety of lobsters and other kinds of seafood, the service is flawless and the atmosphere is perfect for a lively dinner. I would recommend you to have oysters as a starter and then indulge yourself with a fresh lobster. Are you ready to pick your meal from the aquarium inside the restaurant?

40. Enjoy a Jogging Session on the Beach

Local people in Tenerife really love eating and drinking, but they love outdoor activities and sports just as much as their late dinners. Whether they do water sports, yoga or jogging, the beaches are always full of people who exercise. So why not join them?

There is nothing more relaxing than a jogging session on the beach. And you can even finish it with a reinvigorating swim in the cool waters of the ocean.

Ana M. Ionita

At the beach, life is different. Time doesn't move hour to hour but mood to moment. We live by the currents, plan by the tides, and follow the sun.

-Anonymous

Ana M. Ionita

41. Have an Exquisite Brunch

The Concept Boutique & Coffee is a delightful coffee shop in the central area of Santa Cruz. With mouthwatering food, tasty coffee and an interesting clothing store inside, this place is definitely more than a regular café.

This peculiar place puts fashion together with food and drinks creating an interesting mix of visual pleasure and taste desires. Besides being an ideal place for having your morning coffee or a great brunch with your friends, the interesting part is that they also offer an amazing breakfast box you can buy as a present or for yourself. We all deserve to be spoiled once in a while!

42. Have an Adventure: Explore the Charming Masca Village

With an exceptional location, the former pirate village shouldn't be missed when visiting the island. The friendly locals, the delicious food and the breathtaking views make the visit to Masca unforgettable.

And if you want a complete experience adventure yourself into the three hours hiking route from the hamlet through the Masca Barranco to the ocean.

In case you want to have the most peaceful night of your life, spent it in this tiny beautiful village. Not only will the silence overwhelm you, but you will also sleep like a baby.

Just keep in mind that almost nobody cooks after 6 pm, so if you know you usually get hungry in the evening, make sure you have some snacks with you. If you want to try something special in this area, go for the cactus cake.

43. Enjoy a Drink on Avenida Anaga in Santa Cruz

People in Santa Cruz eat dinner late so, the terraces are packed with locals until midnight, almost every day of the week. Many start their working days at 10 am and some have a siesta (midday nap) after lunch, so staying until late is not a problem.

If you want to have dinner like a local, go on Avenida Anaga, a street full of restaurants and bars, as well as night clubs in the weekends, have a few tapas and enjoy a delicious drink.

If you already tried Canarian wine and beer, go for a long drink. Ending a perfect day in the Spanish way, with a tasty gin tonic is a great choice! My personal choice is always Hendrick's Gin with a huge amount of cucumber, but there are many other types you can choose from!

44. Enjoy a Magic Swimming Session at El Tancón

El Tancón is located on the island's west coast and it is one of the most attractive spots on in Tenerife. This amazing cave is definitely a must see!

Also, take your towel and bathing suit and enjoy swimming in the clear waters of the ocean. However, if the ocean is agitated, you should avoid jumping into its waters, because this area is known for being quite dangerous.

45. Eat "Fast Seafood" on the Beach

If you go to the beautiful northern beach, Las Teresitas you should definitely have lunch at one of the beach terraces. Don't expect to be served gourmet food, because everything prepared here is fast and easy.

Order a large beer together with a mixed plate of fried seafood and enjoy a sunny afternoon like a real local. You can either have your food sitting at a table or just grab it and eat it on your towel or sun bed.

After lunch, you can have a perfect nap in the shadow of the charming trees on the beach. This is definitely a fantastic way to spend a lazy Sunday!

46. Have a Special Encounter with the Dolphins

The waters of the Atlantic ocean are full of diverse sea animals. If you want to have a special encounter with some playful dolphins or charming whales you can rent a boat and start sailing. However, if you want to make sure you will see them, an organized trip is a better idea. Locals know exactly where to look for the cute dolphins and whales so you will be taken directly where they " hang out".

But if you want to do it on your own and engage in the adventure of "searching for Flipper" with a rented boat, make sure you have your sailing license with you.

47. Dive into the Blue Waters of the Ocean

Whether you are interested in scuba diving or free diving, Tenerife is the place where you can enjoy both activities. All you need is some courage because the instructors will take care of everything else.

There are a few great diving centers on the island and you only need to pick one, give them a call send choose a date. Of course, you need to be healthy and demonstrate you have no heart problems, breathing issues or a disease that would make diving dangerous or life threatening.

I overcame my deep water fear and completely fell in love with free diving thanks to the great instructors at ApneaCanarias, in Radazul, a town in the northern part of the island.

48. Eat the Best Sushi in Town

Made with fresh fish and delicious ingredients, the sushi served at Fujiyama is among the best I have ever eaten. The restaurant is located in the center of Santa Cruz and it is one the high-end restaurants on the island. The staff is very friendly, helpful and professional.

Besides sushi, I would also recommend the delicious Miso Soup, as well as my favorite main course, the sweet and sour duck. In addition, they have great wine and a delicious coffee.

49. Savor a Delicios Barraquito

Canarian people love their coffee, no matter, if it's 7, am or 9 pm. They drink it in a diversity of ways and one of them is known as "barraquito". Tenerife is actually the capital of barraquito, so coming to the island and not having this delicious coffee is not recommended.

Barraquito is served in a transparent glass and it's made with coffee, hot milk, condensed milk, lemon zest, cinnamon and Tía María or 43 liquor. It is strong and sweet, with a little alcoholic twist! Delicious!

Another type of coffee you can drink here is Café leche leche, which is the name for coffee with milk and condensed milk. The majority of people drink café cortado, which is a shot of coffee with milk.

50. Spend a Romantic Evening Gazing at the Stars

Greenwich used to be a great place for observing the stars, but because of massive pollution the sky is less clear and observing the stars impossible.

Now, with the cleanest sky in Europe, the Canary Islands make a perfect place for this interesting activity. The island has been hosting one of the world's leading observatories, the Canarian Institute of Astrophysics since 1975.

Whether you choose to gaze at the shining stars from a secluded beach or you prefer to go up the mountain to be closer to the sky, your encounter with the clear night sky in Tenerife will be unforgettable.

Ana M. Ionita

Top Reasons to Book This Trip

- **Beaches**: The beauty of the beaches in Tenerife is known all over the world. Not only is the island famous for its black volcanic shores, but there are also beaches with golden sands as well as many charming pebble beaches.

- **Food**: The culinary experiences offered by the multitude of great restaurants in Tenerife creates the perfect destinations for foodies from all over the world.

- **Island Culture**: With incredible historical spots, amazing stories and interesting customs, Tenerife presents its visitors an impressive and rich heritage of tradition.

Ana M. Ionita

> TOURIST

GREATER THAN A TOURIST

Visit GreaterThanATourist.com
http://GreaterThanATourist.com

Sign up for the Greater Than a Tourist
Newsletter
http://eepurl.com/cxspyf

Follow us on Facebook:
https://www.facebook.com/GreaterThanATourist

Follow us on Pinterest:
http://pinterest.com/GreaterThanATourist

Follow us on Instagram:
http://Instagram.com/GreaterThanATourist

Ana M. Ionita

> TOURIST

GREATER THAN A TOURIST

Please leave your honest review of this book on Amazon and Goodreads. Thank you.

We appreciate your positive and negative feedback as we try to provide tourist guidance in their next trip from a local.

> TOURIST

GREATER THAN A TOURIST

You can find Greater Than a Tourist books on Amazon.

Ana M. Ionita

> TOURIST

GREATER THAN A TOURIST

WHERE WILL YOU TRAVEL TO NEXT?

Ana M. Ionita

> TOURIST

GREATER THAN A TOURIST

Our Story

Traveling is a passion of this series creator. She studied abroad in college, and for their honeymoon Lisa and her husband toured Europe. During her travels to Malta, an older man tried to give her some advice based on his own experience living on the island since he was a young boy. She thought he was just trying to sell her something. When traveling to some places she was wary to talk to locals because she was afraid that they weren't being genuine. She created this book series to give you as a tourist an inside view on the place you are exploring and the ability to learn what locals would like to tell tourist. A topic that they are very passionate about.

Ana M. Ionita

> TOURIST

GREATER THAN A TOURIST

Notes

Made in the USA
Middletown, DE
08 November 2018